101 Coo.

MW01090045

in Vietnam

Introduction

So you're going to Vietnam, huh? You lucky lucky thing! You are sure in for a treat because Vietnam is truly one of the most magical countries on this planet. There's a mix of ancient temples, incredible street food, outdoor activities, and shopping that makes Vietnam one of the most enduringly popular tourist destinations on the planet.

In this guide, we'll be giving you the low down on:
- the very best things to shove in your pie hole, from street food staples like heaping bowls of pho, to gourmet restaurants in Saigon
- incredible adventure activities, from white water rafting in rivers to climbing the tallest mountain in all of Indochina
- the best shopping so that you can take a little piece of Vietnam back home with you, whether that's in the form of a handcrafted quilt or a bottle of Scorpion wine
- the coolest historical and cultural sights that you simply cannot afford to miss, from the Temple of Literature to pagodas set into limestone mountains
- where to party like a local person and make Vietnamese friends
- and tonnes more coolness besides!

Let's not waste any more time – here are the 101 coolest things not to miss in Vietnam!

1. Have Clothes Made for You in Hoi An

Hoi An is a small city in central Vietnam that has so much going for it. It has an incredible dining culture, it's perfectly picturesque, and it has beautiful beaches too. But if you are somewhat of a fashionista, you need to know about Hoi An because it's the tailoring capital of Asia. You can have suits, shirts, dresses, shoes, and any other tailored garment made just for you, to a really high quality, and at a rock bottom price to boot.

2. Sip on Fresh Beer on the Street

If you're a beer lover, you'd probably associate places in Europe such as Germany or Czech Republic with delicious beers, but actually, Vietnam also has an incredible beer culture. In the north and central parts of the country, there is such a thing as fresh beer. It is very light, brewed and sold on the same day, and it costs just pennies to purchase a glass of the good stuff. Hanoi and Hoi An are two particularly wonderful places for fresh beer.

3. Eat Endless Bowls of Pho for Breakfast

What do you normally eat for breakfast? A bowl of cereal? Pancakes? Waffles and bacon? Well, you'll find none of that in Vietnam where the most common breakfast is Pho. If you've not heard of Pho before, it's a bowl of soupy, meaty noodles. You might have never had a bowl of noodles for breakfast before, but once you start, a sad piece of toast and jam will never be the same again.

4. Hike Through the Hills of Sapa ✓

Vietnam is an incredibly diverse country. One day you'll be dodging traffic in Saigon and the next you could be taking in the most breath taking views on hikes in the mountains. If you are an outdoorsy person, you will love a town in the north called Sapa. In Sapa, you'll find dramatic mountains, beautiful rice fields, and lots of hill tribes who still have a traditional way of life. Hiking is big news here, and you'll find plenty of tour guides who will share their town with you.

5. Stay on a Houseboat in Ha Long Bay ✓

Ha Long Bay is one of the most iconic sights in the whole country, an archipelago that is made up of almost 2000 islands, most of which are uninhabited. There are so many boat tours that will navigate you through the waters of the bay that you'll have no problems accessing this world famous sight, but if you want to have an extra special trip, you can arrange to stay on a houseboat on the trip. This means that you'll have more time to navigate the waters, you can enjoy the stillness of the bay at night, and you can enjoy a beautiful sunset and sunrise from the comfort of your boat.

6. Sip on Coffee Made From Weasel Dung

Coffee is a big deal in Vietnam, but in between the cups of strong coffee with condensed milk that you'll find on the streets, there is a coffee culture that is altogether more strange. In Hanoi, coffee made from weasel dung is a specialty. Yup, weasel dung. The idea is that the weasels sniff out the freshest and purest coffee beans with their highly sensitive sense of smell, they eat the beans, and then the faeces is used to make the most delicious cup of coffee you'll ever taste. Apparently.

7. Explore the Red Sand Dunes of Mui Ne

Vietnam is a beautiful country that is full of outdoor adventures, and one of the towns that you won't want to miss is called Mui Ne. This is a coastal town, so it's a place where you can get some epic beach time, but even better than that, it's a place where you can find some of the most stunning sand dunes in the world. The red colour of the dunes makes it seem like you're in the Sahara Desert, and the best way to explore is via your own dune buggy.

8. Enjoy the Festivities of the Lunar New Year ✓

Without a doubt, the most important festivity on the Vietnamese calendar is the lunar new year, known in Vietnam as Tet. It usually takes place in late January or early February, and there are many customs associated with the festival. Children receive money in a red envelope from their elders, there will be parades in the streets with a lot of music, drummers, dancers, and masks, and there are traditional decorations in the house, such as bonsais, chrysanthemums, and marigolds.

9. Explore the World's Largest Cave in Phong Nha ✓

Vietnam is a country with many spectacular natural attractions, but did you know that it plays host to the world's largest cave? Yup, Hang Son Doong cave has a height of more than 200 metres, and it's so humungous that it has its own river, jungle, and climate. The cave only opened in 2013, only 500 people are allowed to trek through it each year, and the cost to do so is not cheap at $3000. But if you are looking for an experience like no other, it could be well worth the investment – just be sure to book your place well in advance!

10. Take in a Traditional Water Puppet Show ✓

Vietnam is a country with long and beautiful traditions, and one of these, the water puppet show, is something that is still very popular today. These shows date way back to the 11th century, and wooden puppets appear in a pool of shallow water and act out old Vietnamese tales. Up to eight puppeteers at a time can be standing behind a screen and operating the puppets. Today, you can find the best shows at the Thang Long Water Puppet Theatre in the north of the country.

11. Ease Your Muscles in Kim Boi Hot Spring

After all the sightseeing that you will be doing in Vietnam, you'll probably want a couple of days at the end of your trip when you can simply relax and ease the muscles in your tired legs. For this, we totally recommend Kim Boi hot spring. Clean, mineral water continually emanates from the fountains at a temperature of around 35 degrees, which is a very relaxing bath temperature. The water also has properties that can help with rheumatism and high blood pressure.

12. Visit a Former Prison in Hanoi ✓

The Vietnam War is an extremely sad part of the country's history, but while you are in Vietnam, it's well worth exploring the difficult to subject to really understand what life was like in that time. One of the best places to do this is at the Hao Lo Prison in Hanoi. The former prison complex was built by the French in 1896, but it is most famous for holding American prisoners of war during the Vietnam War.

13. Buy a Handcrafted Quilt at Mekong+

If you are looking for something really special to take back home with you that will always remind you of your trip to Vietnam, a trip to Mekong+ is in order. This social enterprise and store is located in Saigon, Hanoi, and Hoi An, so there is no excuse not to find the time to pop in. They specialise in hand crafted quilts, which are made by women in the rural communities of Vietnam. The enterprise employs more than 340 women, so it's a great way to support local trade and to buy something beautiful at the same time.

14. Get Colourful at Dalat Flower Festival ✓

Vietnam is a very colourful country as it is but it becomes even more so every couple of years when the Dalat Flower Festival is hosted in the city of Dalat. This city is located at a great altitude, and that means it is milder and fresher than most places in Vietnam, making it the ideal place for all kinds of beautiful flowers to bloom. At the festival, you can, of course, see many beautiful garden and flower displays, but there are also music and dance performances.

15. Indulge in Fresh Summer Rolls

The climate in Vietnam can be extremely hot and humid. As a result, a lot of the traditional Vietnamese dishes are designed to be cooling and fresh, and you can't get much fresher than a plateful of delicious fresh summer rolls. Traditionally these rolls are filled up with big fat prawns, rice noodles, and handfuls of fresh herbs such as cilantro. They are wrapped up in rice paper and then dipped into a sweet and spicy sauce.

16. Feel the French Influence at the Saigon ✓ Cathedral of Notre Dame

The Cathedral of Notre Dame is an iconic sight in Paris, right? You would be correct for thinking that, but there is also a Cathedral of Notre Dame in Saigon. Of course, this building was built by the French during colonial rule. It is an absolutely stunning structure with 40 metre high towers in a Roman-esque style that are topped by iron spires. And it doesn't just look pretty – the cathedral is functional with a mass service every Sunday morning.

17. Explore a Traditional Pottery Village

To really get to grips with a country and its culture, you have to know about its arts and crafts traditions, and many people may not realise that Vietnam has an incredible ceramics culture that dates back for centuries. In the village of Bat Trang, which lies just outside of Hanoi, ceramics is the bread and butter of everyone living there. Stroll through and you will be invited to observe the locals making pottery, and you can even have a go on the potters' wheel yourself. Buying something from Bat Trang will also be much better than anything you can buy in a souvenir shop.

18. Try Vietnamese Comfort Food, Banh Xeo

When you think of Vietnamese food, you probably think of very fresh dishes such as summer rolls, but if it is comfort food that you are after, you absolutely need to try Banh Xeo. It translates literally as sizzling cake, and the dish is essentially a savoury fried pancake made with rice flour and turmeric, and it can be stuffed with shrimps, fatty pork, bean sprouts, and lots of herbs. Banh Xeo is a major street food favourite in Saigon.

19. Explore an Authentic Hill Tribe's Market

Bac Ha is a sleepy town in the hills of Vietnam close to the Chinese border. But this sleepy place seriously wakes up every Sunday when it hosts a very colourful Sunday market. This is the main market for lots of hill tribes in the surrounding villages and towns, and the population more than doubles on a Sunday when people descend upon Bac Ha to buy everything they need for the week ahead. You'll be able to find local arts and crafts, flowers, food, and even livestock.

20. Have the Local Experience With Couchsurfing

When you travel to a country like Vietnam that is so different it can be all too easy to do the safe, touristy things, but that will only show you a small glimmer of the country. Ditch the western restaurants and posh hotels for a little bit and have a Couchsurfing experience instead. This is a website where people with spare beds and couches invite foreigners into their home. Yes, you can save money this way, but it's the cultural exchange that is the really valuable part.

21. Visit a Floating Market on the Mekong Delta ✓

When you think of floating markets in Asia, Thailand and the floating markets in Bangkok probably first come to mind. But there are also beautiful floating markets along the Mekong River in the south of Vietnam. Phong Dien Market outside of Can Tho is probably the most famous of them all. You'll find row boats selling all kinds of foods, and if you want to experience the market at its best, you should get up early and try and make it there between 5 and 7 in the morning.

22. Celebrate the Coastal Festival of Cau Ngu

Cau Ngu Festival is one of the most unique festivals that you will find anywhere in the country. It is otherwise known as the Whale Festival, and it's the most important festival of the year for the fisherman of Da Nang. They believe the whale to be a very special creature, and the festival pays homage to the sea mammal. During the festival, locals worship the whale, and they also engage in fishing, and play games.

23. Get to Grips With Village Life in Sinho

If you want to have an "off the beaten" track experience while you're in Vietnam, you can't do much better than the peaceful mountain village of Sinho, which is located in the north of the country. There is literally just one hotel in the whole area, Thanh Binh Hotel, so you will definitely have the local experience when you arrive there. Instead of the tourist markets loaded with handicrafts, here you are more likely to be confronted with livestock and very little spoken English – but that's all part of the fun!

24. Enjoy Coffee With a View at Eon Café

Because of the frantic pace of Saigon, it can be hard to appreciate just how beautiful the city can be from the ground. But one place where you can appreciate an incredible vista of the whole city and its liveliness in action is the Eon Café. What makes this café special is that it's located in the tallest building in all of Vietnam, the Bitexco Tower, and as it's located on the 50th, 51st, and 52nd floors, so you are sure to get the most epic view of the city while you are sipping on your latte.

25. Allow Ban Gioc Waterfall to Take Your Breath Away

Everybody loves a waterfall, and if the idea of spending a day relaxing at a waterfall with a picnic sounds like a good time to you, you'll simply be bowled away by the epic Ban Gioc waterfall. This is one of the best known sites in the country, and its waters are fed by the Quy Son River. You can hire local people to take you in rafts up the river and witness the waterfall so close that you can feel the spray of it. There is also a natural pool there that you are welcome to splash around in.

26. Visit a 6ᵗʰ Century Pagoda in Hanoi

If historic attractions are what you're after, you can't do much better than a morning exploring the Tran Quoc Pagoda in Hanoi. This is the oldest Buddhist temple in the whole city, dating back to the 11ᵗʰ century, and it's located on a small island in a lake, which makes the experience of visiting the pagoda that much more special. On the grounds, you can also find a cutting from the same Bodhi tree under which the Buddha sat and meditated.

27. Trek Through Cuc Phuong National Park √

If you are the kind of person who goes on holiday to get away from the stresses of urban life and to immerse yourself in the quietude of nature, you will certainly want to know about Cuc Phuong National Park, which is the country's largest national park. Inside the park you will find an endangered primate rescue centre, beautiful botanical gardens, a turtle conservation centre, and dozens of trails that make it easy for you to trek through the greenery.

28. Try a Half Hatched Duck Egg

If you fancy yourself as something of a food adventurer, there are plenty of weird and wonderful things that you'll be able to sample in Vietnam. A half hatched duck egg is one of them. That isn't a euphemism or a metaphor, we are literally talking about a half formed foetal egg here. They are actually more of a medicinal thing as they are said to be very useful for women who have given birth and want to restore their strength. But if you fancy trying something new and a little odd, this could be just the ticket.

29. Watch Traditional Vietnamese Dance in Saigon ✓

Vietnam is a country with more than fifty ethnic tribes. Because of this, there are thousands of traditions from the tribes that reach back for centuries. Dance is a very important part of the traditional culture, and while in Saigon, you should definitely make the effort to catch a dance show in one of the theatres. One of the best dance shows is called The Mist. It tells the story of traditional Vietnamese life through incredible dance performances.

30. Get Some Greenery at Saigon Botanical Gardens ✓

Saigon is an epic city, but for some people it can be very overwhelming. The buildings are tall, the traffic is constant, and there is hustle and bustle everywhere. If you need a place inside the city to get away from it all, the Saigon Botanical Gardens will be just what you are looking for. There are more than 1800 types of tree and over 230 types of plants inside the gardens, which were created more than a century ago.

31. Discover Ancient Artefacts at the Museum of Vietnamese History ✓

There are lots of museums around the country where you can learn about the Vietnam War, but what if you want to get a glimpse into Ancient Vietnamese History? The Museum of Vietnamese History in Saigon is the perfect place. There is an astounding number of items, and highlights include artefacts from the Bronze Age Dong Son civilisation, which dates back to 2000 BC, and the Funan civilisation. History buffs will be enamoured.

32. Dine in the Dark in Saigon ✓

It's true that the street food of Vietnam is some of the best you will find in the world, but there are times when you will want to swap your plastic street stool for a comfortable seat at a restaurant table. If you are looking for a dining experience with a bit of a difference in Saigon, NOIR, a dining in the dark restaurant could be right up your alley. It's a unique experience but it's not just a gimmick – the food and wine menu is actually fantastic.

33. Go Snorkelling on the Cham Islands

Vietnam is a country with a whole lot of coastline and so it's the perfect destination for beach lovers. But if you are not the kind of person who can spend endless days sunbathing, you might be wondering what other beach activities you can try your hand at to occupy your time? Well, the Cham Islands are the centre of diving and snorkelling in Vietnam. There are 135 species of coral around the islands and a lot of sea life too so this is the perfect spot for an unforgettable underwater adventure.

34. Have a Relaxing Day at An Bang Beach

When travellers head to Hoi An, as so many of them do, they often stick to the very picturesque town, and limit their stay for a few days just to get some clothes tailored. While there is absolutely nothing wrong with that, this really underestimates how beautiful the beaches are in Hoi An. Most of the guesthouses are not located right on the beach, but you can rent a bicycle and cycle to the beach in 20 minutes quite easily. An Bang is our favourite of the Hoi An beaches. It's laid back, has calm waters, and there are lovely beach restaurants too.

35. Sip on Tea in a Hoi An Teahouse

If you find yourself in Hoi An and you aren't sure what to do in between having clothes tailored and eating delicious meals, we highly recommend a trip to Reaching Out Teahouse. The whole place is managed by women who have hearing difficulties and it is forbidden to make any noise while you are inside the tea house. Order a tea tasting or a coffee tasting menu and you might find, perhaps for the first time ever, that you can really appreciate the taste of a fragrant cup of tea without the distraction of chatter and conversation.

36. Enjoy a Cable Car Ride Over the Hills of Dalat

Dalat is definitely one of the more underrated locations of Vietnam. Sure, it doesn't have the museums of Hanoi or the crazy nightlife of Saigon, but it's a great place to kick back where there is a slightly cooler temperature. Dalat is also a very attractive small city, and one of the best ways to get a vista of the whole place is via the city's own cable car system. The cable car will also take you to a beautiful pagoda on a hilltop.

37. Have Fun at a Hill Tribe Harvest Festival

In the hills of Vietnam, almost everybody is employed in agriculture, and this makes harvest time one of the most special moments of the year. If you can, be sure to check out an authentic hill tribe harvest festival, like the one in the small town of Co Tu. Although the town is small, the turnout is staggeringly huge. You can expect traditional dancing, chanting, lots of dressing up, and a blood sacrifice of a pig or a buffalo, which is something that vegetarians may have to close their eyes for.

38. Chow Down on White Roses

One of the loveliest things about Vietnam is that as you travel around the different regions and cities in the country, you can try different types of foods, because each place has its own distinct food culture. When you are in the lovely town of Hoi An, you'll want to find the local eateries and markets where you'll find something called white roses. These are dumplings made with shrimp that are then wrapped in rice pepper and covered in flakes of crispy garlic, and they are delicious.

39. Discover Cham Art in Da Nang ✓

The Cham people are an indigenous group in the country whose roots date back to the 2nd century. They have their own traditional cultures, and you can explore Cham art in the Museum of Cham Sculpture in the coastal town of Da Nang.

This museum actually has the world's largest collection of Cham artefacts, including altars, lingas, garudas, and images of Shiva, Brahma and Vishnu that all date way back to a period in between the 5th and 15th centuries.

40. Visit Doi Tam Drum Village

In Vietnam, there are various towns and villages dotted around the rural parts of the country that are dedicated to niche areas of craft making. Head to Doi Tam, which is located in the northern part of the country, and you will find a village that has been dedicated to drum making for around 1000 years. Children in the village are taught the profession from as early on as five years of age, and you'll have the chance to see the drums being made for yourself if you visit the village.

41. Hike Up Lang Bian Mountain

Are you the kind of person who likes to get active on holiday? If so, you'll be glad to know that there are a tonne of mountains that you can climb in Vietnam. The nice thing about Lang Biang mountain is that you don't have to commit to a long trek as most people can get to the top of the mountain within about three hours. The trek is steep so you should have a certain fitness level, but the smell of pines as you walk, and the vista from the top will be more than worth it.

42. Eat a Comforting Bowl of Chao Ga

If comfort food is your thing, you'll want to dodge the fresh spring rolls and herb filled bowls of pho and instead you should try something called Chao Ga. This is essentially a bowl of Chicken porridge. It might not sound that appealing, but that's only because you haven't tried it before. It's actually a delicious and comforting dish filled with huge hulks of chicken. It can be thought of as the Vietnamese equivalent of chicken soup and it's perfect for when you need something restorative.

43. Motorcycle from Hanoi to Saigon

One of the less appealing parts of travel in southeast Asia is having to squeeze up to five people on a three person bench on a 12 hour bus ride. But there is an alternative. In Vietnam, there are scores of backpackers who choose to rent motorcycles and power their way from Hanoi to Saigon. This obviously isn't a journey to do in one go, but it's a great way to travel at your own pace and take in towns such as Hue, Hoi An, and Mui Ne on route.

44. Dive in the Waters of Phu Quoc

Phu Quoc is without a doubt one of the most beautiful places in all of Vietnam. If it is island paradise that you are looking for, Phu Quoc looks like a postcard with white sand beaches and crystal clear waters. But as well as picturesque beaches, you should know that there is also a whole lot of beauty under the sea. For this reason, the island is extremely popular with divers, whether they are total beginners or more experienced. Under the sea, you'll find turtles, barracudas, and many other tropical species.

45. Kayak Around the Islands of Ha Long Bay ✓

Most people are aware that Ha Long Bay is one of the most beautiful spots in all of the Vietnam, and it definitely warrants a visit. But instead of going on a big tour on a huge boat, a better way of exploring the bay is by kayaking around it. There are many tour companies that can arrange this, and it's so much better because you get to explore at your own pace and you get to explore under arches and through islets that are actually inaccessible by boats.

46. Party Hard at Lush Nightclub

If you are a party person who loves to shimmy on the dancefloor, the capital city, Saigon, is 100% the place that you need to be in Vietnam. There are numerous bar and clubbing options, but our favourite has to be Lush Nightclub. At Lush, hip-hop or dance tunes blare out of the speakers seven nights a week, and there is an outdoor deck where you can cool off a little after dancing all night long.

47. Learn About Vietnamese Ethnic Groups in Hanoi

Hopping from city to city in Vietnam is really fun, but when you are in the cities of the country, it is hard to get to grips with all of the different ethnic groups and hill tribes in Vietnam. Fortunately, in Hanoi there is a really wonderful museum dedicated to the ethnology of the country, the Museum of Ethnology. In the museum, you'll find tribal art, household objects, and everyday artefacts from many different tribes around the country.

48. Explore the Cu Chi Tunnels

Not heard of the Cu Chi Tunnels before? Well, these are a network or underground, interlinked tunnels that were used during the Vietnamese military option in the Vietnam war, and were an essential part of the country's defence. The tunnels have been preserved, and these days part of them are a major tourist attraction. On your visit, you'll be able to discover secret meeting rooms, you can walk through the tunnels, and you can even sample a meal that a soldier would have eaten.

49. Be Wowed by Pongour Waterfall

If it's waterfalls that you are into, you will love the Dalat area of the country, which is home to many of them. We think that the most special of the bunch is Pongour Falls. The really nice thing about this particular waterfall is that you can climb up all seven tiers and bathe in the water in each one of them. This makes Pongour a place where you can easily spend the whole day splashing around.

50. Try a Vietnamese Hamburger, Bun Cha

Yes, sampling all of the local foods in a foreign country is awesome, but sometimes you just want to chow down on a juicy hamburger. Fortunately, in Vietnam you can have the best of both worlds because one of the local dishes, Bun Cha, is kind of like the Vietnamese version of a burger. Bun Cha is essentially flavoured and grilled pork, but instead of it being served on a bun, you'll have it served on noodles and with a dipping sauce.

51. Get Back to Nature in Ba Be National Park ✓

If it's nature that you are after, Vietnam has absolutely tonnes of it, and one of the best places to feel a connection with the serenity and beauty of the natural world in Vietnam is at Ba Be National Park. The great thing about this park is that it has a bit of everything. There are towering limestones mountains, evergreen forests, gorges and caves, and serene lakes. There's also hundreds of wildlife species here, including the Burmese python.

52. Send Home a Postcard From Saigon's Central Post Office

A post office is a post office is a post office, right? Wrong. The post office in Saigon is one of the most famous and iconic buildings in the city, and it's with good reason. It's actually one of the most classic pieces of French architecture in Saigon, designed by Gustav Eiffel, the guy who is responsible for the Eiffel Tower. The post office is also still fully functional so you are free to pop in at any time and send a postcard back to your grandmother.

53. Dent Your Wallet at Hanoi Night Market

All across southeast Asia, there is an incredible market culture, and Vietnam is certainly no exception. When you are in the northern city of Hanoi, a great way to pass the evenings is to stroll through Hanoi Night Market. This is a place to buy arts and crafts and Vietnamese fashion accessories. Just be sure to haggle because the first price asked of you will be highly inflated!

54. Start Spring With Bai Dinh Pagoda Festival

If you really want to experience the beautiful traditions of Vietnam, you have to join in with the local celebrations, and the Bai Dinh Pagoda Festival is one that is particularly fun. It is hosted every year in Sinh Duoc village on the sixth day of the first lunar month. The festival is hosted to worship the Buddha and also to honour historic events. Locals spend months beforehand preparing floats and costumes for the epic parade, and there are also activities such as wrestling during the festival.

55. Eat the Vietnamese Baguette, Banh Mi

If you are travelling around southeast Asia, you'll soon notice that there is not so much of a bread culture. In Vietnam, noodles are certainly more popular, but you can still find fluffy bread thanks to the country's French influence. If you love nothing more than to chow down on a crusty baguette, you'll love Banh Mi, which is essentially the Vietnamese version of this. Inside, you will typically find sliced pork, liver pate, pickled vegetables, and sprinklings of cilantro.

56. Get Away From it All in Scenic Mai Chau

The cities of Vietnam are fantastic, but they are very busy and can be more than a little stressful. If you want to get out of the city and need a place to relax, you should seriously consider the small village of Mai Chau. While in Mai Chau, you will be surrounded by the most dramatic towering cliffs, and beautiful fields of green all around you. There is little to do other than walk around, eat, and enjoy a very relaxed pace of life – and that's the whole beauty of the place.

57. Learn About Vietnamese Women in Hanoi

Hanoi is a museum lover's paradise, and one of the very best museums there is the Vietnamese Women's Museum. The museum showcases the important role that women have played and still play in Vietnamese society. Some of the highlights from the incredible displays include ancient cooking utensils, Vietnamese women's fashion through the ages, and traditional craft items such as woven baskets and ceramics.

58. Learn a Bit of Vietnamese

When you visit any new country, the best way of connecting with the local people and having a really authentic experience is to learn the language. Okay, if you're in the country for a week it may not be that feasible, but if your trip is longer, learning a little bit of Vietnamese could really transform your vacation experience. We can recommend Hidden Hanoi Language School in Hanoi where there are lessons geared to visiting foreigners.

59. Feel the Hustle and Bustle of Binh Tay Market

In Vietnam, market culture is everything, and there are more than a few impressive markets in the capital city of Saigon. Perhaps the most impressive of them all is Binh Tay Market. At Binh Tay Market, you will find everything under the sun. Whether you want to find cheap electronics, handicrafts to take back with you, traditional clothing, or just a filling Vietnamese breakfast, you'll find it all here and then some.

60. Get Festive at Giong Festival in Hanoi

Going Festival is an annual festival that takes place all around the city of Hanoi every springtime in order to celebrate Saint Giong, who is one of the most important figures in Vietnamese mythology, and displayed merit in protecting the country against foreign enemies. Throughout the festival, you will see many people offering bamboo flowers to the saint, and you may witness a reproduction of the slaying of the invaders.

61. Go Fishing in Nha Trang Bay

Nha Trang is a very popular beach destination on Vietnam's coast, but if you'd rather be out in the water than on the beach, perhaps you should try one of the popular fishing expeditions there. The fish here are plentiful and even complete beginners can have great luck in the waters, sometimes even catching large fish like red snapper. You can then grill your fish in the evening and enjoy a fresh seafood supper!

62. Have a Suction Cups Massage

One of the very best things about travelling in southeast Asia is that massages can be found at a rock bottom price and they are mostly of an extremely high quality. But instead of having a traditional massage on your travels in Vietnam, why not try something a little bit different? You will also be able to find a "cupping massage" around the country. This massage uses suction cups to create local suction points on the skin, which is said to improve circulation and balance of the body's elements.

63. Learn About Fish Sauce on Phu Quoc

As you travel around Vietnam, you may notice a pungent smell in the air wherever there is a street food stall. That smell is probably fish sauce, and it is used in a huge assortment of dishes in Vietnam and southeast Asia. Well, if you visit the island of Phu Quoc and you are tired of endless beach days, you can visit a fish sauce factory there. Guides are available to show you the process of fish sauce making in the factory, and, of course, you should take a few bottles home with you.

64. Visit the Snake Village, Le Mat

The small village of Le Mat lies just 7 kilometres outside of Hanoi but everything about it is a world away from the big city, not least because this is a "snake village". Basically, if you are feeling brave, this is the place to come and eat snake. You can choose the snake to eat, and then the blood and bile will be drained, which you can gulp down with rice wine. The meat can then be added to soups, skewers, and spring rolls. Are you brave enough?

65. Go White Water Rafting in Dalat

Do you fancy yourself as something of an adventurer? In that case, you'll not only want to look at the beautiful nature of Vietnam, but actually have thrilling experiences inside it. In and around Dalat, the terrain lends itself to outdoor adventures like trekking, canyoning, and biking, but the thing we love the most is the white water rafting. The Langbian River is perfect because there are moments when the river is ferocious and moments when it is calmer so you can have an adventure, but also catch your breath and take in the scenery.

66. Sip on Scorpion Wine

The local tipple in Vietnam is definitely rice wine. Although it's called wine, it's actually more of a whisky made from fermented rice. A few glasses of the stuff will make you extremely light headed, indeed. An interesting take on the rice wine is snake or scorpion wine. You can probably imagine what this is. Whole snakes and scorpions are infused in the wine to impart their flavour and their nutritional properties. Walk along the street markets, and you'll spot the animals inside the bottles.

67. Learn About Traditional Vietnamese Medicine ✓

There is a handful of really great museums in Saigon, but a lot of them have to do with the war. Important as that is, you might want a different kind of museum experience while you are in the city. The Museum of Traditional Vietnamese Medicine is a place where, you guessed it, you can learn about traditional Vietnamese medicine! The museum covers six floors and has more than 3000 artefacts. You'll be able to see medicinal root slicers, a 2500 year old pestle used for pounding medicines, and much more besides.

68. Swing a Golf Club in Lang Co

If your idea of a really relaxing break is spending numerous days on the golf course, you absolutely shouldn't forget to pack your clubs on your trip to Vietnam. It may not be known as a golfing country, but this is not to say that there are not incredible golf clubs around. Laguna Lang Co Golf Course is actually said to be a favourite place of golfing legend, Nick Faldo. With coast on one side and mountains on the other, it's the most picturesque place you will ever swing a golf club.

69. Pick Yourself Up With a Vietnamese Coffee

Are you a coffee fanatic? If so, your love for Vietnam is going to explode when you try the delicious local coffee in cafes and on the streets. With a traditional cup of Vietnamese coffee, you will normally have an intensely dark and strong brew, which would then be sweetened with a thick glug of condensed milk. Strong, rich, hearty, and sweet – it is everything that a cup of coffee should be.

70. Visit the Many Tombs in Hue ✓

Hue is a small city on the coast of the country located in between Hanoi and Hoi An. It is a beautiful place that is all too often overlooked, and it's particularly great if you want to have a greater sense of the country's impressive history, because it's in Hue that you'll find a selection of Royal Tombs. The Tu Duc Tomb is one of the most elaborately decorated tombs in the country, embedded in a lush pine forest. And the Minh Mang Tomb also has lakes, pavilions, and gardens.

71. Visit the Thien Mu Pagoda

The Thien Mu Pagoda is a temple located in the city of Hue, and at seven stories in height, it is the tallest religious building in the entire country. The construction of the pagoda dates back to 1601, so it's a great place to get a feeling for the country's religious culture, and also its history. There are beautiful gardens surrounding the pagoda, so this is a lovely spot for passing a peaceful afternoon.

72. Understand the Vietnam War at the War Remnants Museum ✓

Amazing!

The War Remnants Museum in Saigon is, without a doubt, one of the most important museums in the country, and it conveys the brutality of war with one hell of a punch. Some of the more disturbing artefacts are photographs of children harmed by the US bombing. You will also be able to find posters and other materials from the anti-war movement worldwide, and a selection of infantry weapons, bombs, and armoured vehicles.

73. Purchase Pearls on Phu Quoc ✓

If it's a beach break that you are after, waste no time in heading to the gorgeous and isolated island of Phu Quoc. But while you are there, you may notice more than white sand and clear waters, because Phu Quoc is also known for its pearls. Walk the streets and you will see pearls sellers everywhere. You get what you pay for, and, of course, there is a huge variety of prices. But this doesn't mean that you shouldn't haggle your way down to a bargain!

74. Stroll the Authentic Dong Xuan Market

In the major tourist places of Vietnam, there are the places where the locals go and the places where the tourists go. If you want the authentic Vietnamese market experience in Hanoi, Dong Xuan Market is well worth a stroll. The market is gargantuan and it pretty much sells everything that you could ever want to purchase. You'll find electronics, handicrafts, household items, food, and tonnes more.

75. Learn How to Cook Like a Local

Anybody who has travelled to Vietnam is sure to tell you that one of the major highlights of their trip was the incredible food. But how much more incredible would it be if you actually learned how to make authentic dishes so you could share them with friends and family at home? Hoi An is one of the best places in the country for both eating and cooking, and we love the class at Red Bridge restaurant. They'll send you to local markets in a boat to buy ingredients and even have their own herb garden on site.

76. Find Something Special in Hang Da Market

Fancy doing some clothes shopping while you're in Vietnam? Well if you like rummaging around markets and finding unique items to wear, you will positively fall head over heels for Hang Da Market, which is located in Hanoi. There is actually more than clothing here, but it's the threads that are the star of the show, and you can find them in the basement. FYI, it's mostly Vietnamese sizes that are catered to so if you're a little larger than average, you may have to rummage extra hard.

77. Take a Cruise Along the Mekong Delta

Vietnam is a country of many contrasts. There are the bustling cities but then the peaceful countryside and small villages along the river. To experience true village life along the Mekong in a relaxed way, it can be a great idea to take a cruise along the Mekong river. There are many tour companies, and you'll be able to visit catfish farms, working floating markets, and take in stunning sunsets from the water.

78. Escape Saigon with a Trip to Binh Quoi Village

Saigon is a wonderful city, but it can also be really full-on. If you are feeling slightly overwhelmed by the country's capital, it's possible to take a break in a village, which is actually located within the city limits. Binh Quoi has been set up as a tourist village within the city by the local government, and inside you can find a 700 seater floating restaurant, beautiful gardens and thatched gardens, and water puppet shows.

79. Take a Walk Through Tan Ky House

If you are wondering what there is to do in Hoi An apart from visiting the beach and having clothes tailored, you should absolutely spend a morning strolling through Tan Ky House. This stunning house was built two centuries ago by an ethnically Vietnamese family and it has been preserved across seven centuries. Be sure to look out for the Japanese and Chinese elements of the architecture and design like the Chinese poems hanging from the roof.

80. Paddle Through the Fairy Stream of Mui Ne

Mui New is the kind of beach destination where you simply relax and take in the beautiful red sand and splash in the warm waters. Something else fun to visit there is the Fairy Stream. The stream has a red colour from the sand beneath and from the reflected light. All around you, you'll be able to see the undulating red sand dunes, and the effect is something altogether magical and romantic that you shouldn't miss.

81. Enjoy Happy Hour at a Saigon Sky Bar

What better way is there to enjoy the incredible city of Saigon than by taking in a cocktail with loved ones at a Sky Bar where you can look out over the whole city? Amazing but expensive, right? Well, actually, it really doesn't have to be, at least not if you make the most of Happy Hour at the Glow Skybar, which lasts from 5pm to 8pm every day. And actually, this is the best time to grab a drink there, because you can catch the epic Saigon sunset while sipping on your drink.

82. Trek to the Top of Mount Fansipan

Mount Fansipan is the highest mountain in Indochina at a height of over 10,000 feet – wow! If you are a real adventurer, there is no greater adventurer in Vietnam than climbing to the top of this epic mountain. There are tour companies that will take you on a three day hike up the mountain so you get to take your time, acclimate to the altitude, and savour the experience. Just be aware that this is no gentle hike – the trek is steep and often strenuous.

83. Celebrate Vietnamese Ancestry on the Anniversary of the Hung Kings

If you want to get to grips with how Vietnam's ancient past affects the present lives of the Vietnamese, you have to be in the country at the time of the Anniversary of the Hung Kings, which takes place on the 10th day of the third lunar month. The festival pays contribution to the Hung Kings, who are the first emperors od Vietnam who founded the nation. People from all over the country visit the Hung King Temple to join with the incredible processions and give their offerings.

84. Learn How to Surf in Da Nang

If laying on the beach all day isn't something that you like to do when you take a vacation, this doesn't mean that you have to skip Vietnam's picturesque beach towns altogether. Da Nang is one place along the coast where it's also possible to take part in exciting activities in the water such as surfing. And it doesn't matter if you are a total beginner. There are tonnes of surf schools along this stretch of coast when you can rent the equipment and be guided until you're a surfing pro!

85. Have an Artsy Day at the Fine Arts Museum

If you want to go on an artsy vacation, you probably think that a trip to Florence or Paris would be better than a trip to Vietnam. But actually, the country has a surprisingly strong arts culture, and nowhere is this more evident than at the Fine Arts Museum in Saigon. This is the primary arts museum in Ho Chi Minh City, and it's a wonderful place to discover the visual arts culture of Vietnam. You can find ancient Buddhist art, Vietnamese ceramics, silk paintings, sculptures, and more besides.

86. Take a Romantic Boat Ride in the Valley of Love

If you find yourself in Dalat for a few days, and particularly if you are visiting with your partner, be sure to etch out some time to visit the Valley of Love. As the name would suggest, this is a supremely romantic place. The highlight is a huge lake that is surrounded by lush gardens. There are swan peddle boats on the lake, which might be a bit cheesy, but we kind of love them for that reason!

87. Watch Weavers Make Baskets in Phu Vinh

If you fancy an interesting day trip outside of Hanoi, the village of Phu Vinh lies just 35km outside of the city, and it is the centre for rattan and bamboo weaving in the country. As you descend upon the village, you are likely to be astounded by the numbers of weavers you see hard at work. A trip here makes a great day learning about a traditional craft, and you can take items such as baskets, lampshades, screens, and ornaments away with you.

88. Indulge a Sweet Tooth With Banh Cam ✓

When you think of Vietnamese foods, you probably think of delicious soupy noodles and fresh seafood, but could you name even one Vietnamese dessert? If you have a sweet tooth, fear not because although they aren't world famous, Vietnam does have desserts, and our favourite is something called Banh Cam. These are basically sweet sesame balls. Glutinous rice flour is deep fried so it has a chewy texture and then it's coated in sweet sesame.

89. Explore the Incredible Marble Mountains

If you are an adventurous kind of person, you will definitely want to get on board with the rugged Marble Mountains, which are located just outside of Da Nang. This cluster of five hills made from limestone and marble contain epic hiking trails, caves, tunnels, and even pilgrimage sites – and they are all waiting to be explored. Ascend to the top and you'll have a killer view over the surrounding area.

90. Zoom Through the Kom Tum Motorbike Loop

Hiring a motorcycle and zooming through the country is a popular activity in Vietnam, but which is the best motorcycle loop that you can do in the country? Well, our favourite is the Kom Tum Loop. This is a 110 kilometre loop that you can get done in a day, and it will take you on a journey through country roads close the Cambodia and Laos borders. You'll see beautiful lakes, Vietnam war sites, and rolling countryside as you motor through.

91. Celebrate the Mid-Autumn Festival in Hoi An

Vietnam is a country with a huge festival culture. No matter what time of year you go to the country, you are likely to find some kind of epic celebration, and if you make it there in the autumn, we highly recommend the Mid-Autumn Festival in

Hoi An. It is held in mid-September after the final rice harvest, and the festival offers a chance to celebrate a good yield and to chase bad spirits away. The highlight of the celebrations is a huge parade with dragon dancers and fire breathers.

92. Relax Around Lak Lake

Lak Lake is the largest freshwater lake in the Central Highlands of Vietnam, and it is surrounded by the most gorgeously serene rural landscapes. If you are not so much of a city person, skip Saigon, and spend more time here instead. There are minority villages around the lake, and in some of these you will find people who can take you out on the lake on a rafting trip. Fun, beautiful, and serene – everything that you could want from a trip to Vietnam's countryside.

93. Watch Rice Paper Being Made

During your time in Vietnam, you will no doubt, and definitely should, tuck into many fresh summer rolls. All of these rolls are covered in rice paper, and if you have the chance, you should visit a small village called Ku Chi Lang where the rice paper is still made according to old traditions. Many of the local people won't mind you watching them do this work. Look out for the rice paper drying on bamboo racks everywhere around the village.

94. Take an Overnight Trip on Quan Lan Island

Everybody knows that Ha Long Bay is one of the moist beautiful places to visit in Vietnam, and you should definitely take the time to visit this magical part of the country, but did you know that some of the islands in the bay are habitable and that you can actually stay on some of the islands? Quan Lan is incredibly picturesque, it has a tiny population, but it's possible to stay there overnight, so it's the perfect place for an overnight trip and to experience Ha Long Bay in a different way.

95. Enjoy Beach Days in Cam Ranh

There is so much to see and do around Vietnam, but if you are a beach lover through and through, you may just want to perch yourself on the finest sandy beach that you can find. If that sounds like you, we can wholeheartedly recommend Cam Ranh. There are miles and miles of unspoiled coast, and yet somehow it isn't quite on the tourist radar yet. The best thing to do here is splash in the crystal clear water, top up your tan, and eat at seafood shacks on the sand. And what else could you possibly need?

96. Take in a Show at Hanoi Opera House ✓

Hanoi is a city with a lot of gorgeous buildings from the French colonial period, and the Hanoi Opera House is one of them. It was built in the early twentieth century, and has a very European style with Italian marble throughout and copper chandeliers. These days, the Opera House is still in use, and if you fancy a night of getting dressed up, it's a great idea to catch a show here. The shows by the Vietnamese National Orchestra are always spellbinding.

97. Purchase Unique Souvenirs at Saigon Kitsch

Souvenir shopping can be a massive stress, but not in Vietnam. There is so much beauty all around and so many handicrafts that you'll have to figure out what not to buy. But if your tastes are somewhat more contemporary, be sure to pay a visit to Saigon Kitsch. This store in the capital city specialises in items such as reproductions of propaganda posters and laptop and tablet covers made from recycled local packaging.

98. Take it Easy at Kenh Ga Hot Spring

Vietnam is blessed to be a country full of incredible natural resources. You can experience this more than anywhere at the Kenh Ga Hot Spring. The natural mineral water here flows from a mountain top and has a consistent temperature of about 53 degrees – definitely warm enough to ease your weary muscles. As well as being very relaxing, the mineral properties of the water are said to help with arthritis and skin conditions.

99. Chow Down on Dried Buffalo Meat in Ha Giang

As you travel around Vietnam, you will notice that there are local culinary specialities in the different cities, towns, and villages that you visit. Ha Giang is a province at the very north of the country where Vietnam borders China. The specialty of the region is dried buffalo meat. The meat is first marinated in ginger, chilli, and other local spices, and it is then left out to dry in strings for a long time until it is ready for you to eat.

100. Take A Day Trip to the Perfume Pagoda

The Perfume Pagoda is one of the most iconic Buddhist temple complexes in the whole country, located around 60km south of Hanoi. Getting there isn't easy. First you have to travel by road, then on the river, and then by foot – but the scenery on the way is incredible, and you'll be rewarded once you arrive. The shrines are built into the limestone mountains themselves. If you want an extra special visit, go there for the Huong Pagoda Festival, when thousands of Vietnamese people make a pilgrimage to the shrines.

101. Feel Vietnam's History at the Temple of Literature

The Temple of Literature is one of the most important sites in the country. It was built in the 11th century as a university dedicated to Confucius, and since then thousands upon thousands of important Vietnamese scholars have graduated from the university. The "temple" now functions as a memorial to education and literature. Inside you'll find gardens, a pavilion, and a lake. A must visit in Hanoi.

Before You Go...

Hey you! Thanks so much for reading **101 Coolest Things to Do in Vietnam**. We really hope that this helps to make your time in Vietnam the most fun and memorable trip that it can be. And if you enjoyed reading the book, it would be super cool if you could leave a review on the book's Amazon web page. You're awesome – thank you!

Keep your eyes peeled on www.101coolestthings.com and have an amazing trip!

The 101 Coolest Things Team

Made in the USA
San Bernardino, CA
31 October 2016